Usborne
Bible Stories
for Little Children

Usborne

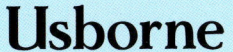

Bible Stories
for Little Children

Retold by Phillip Clarke and Kirsteen Robson
Illustrated by BlueBean, Héloïse Mab, Katya Longhi, Erin Brown, Corinne Caro and Can Tuğrul
Designed by Hope Reynolds
Edited by Lesley Sims

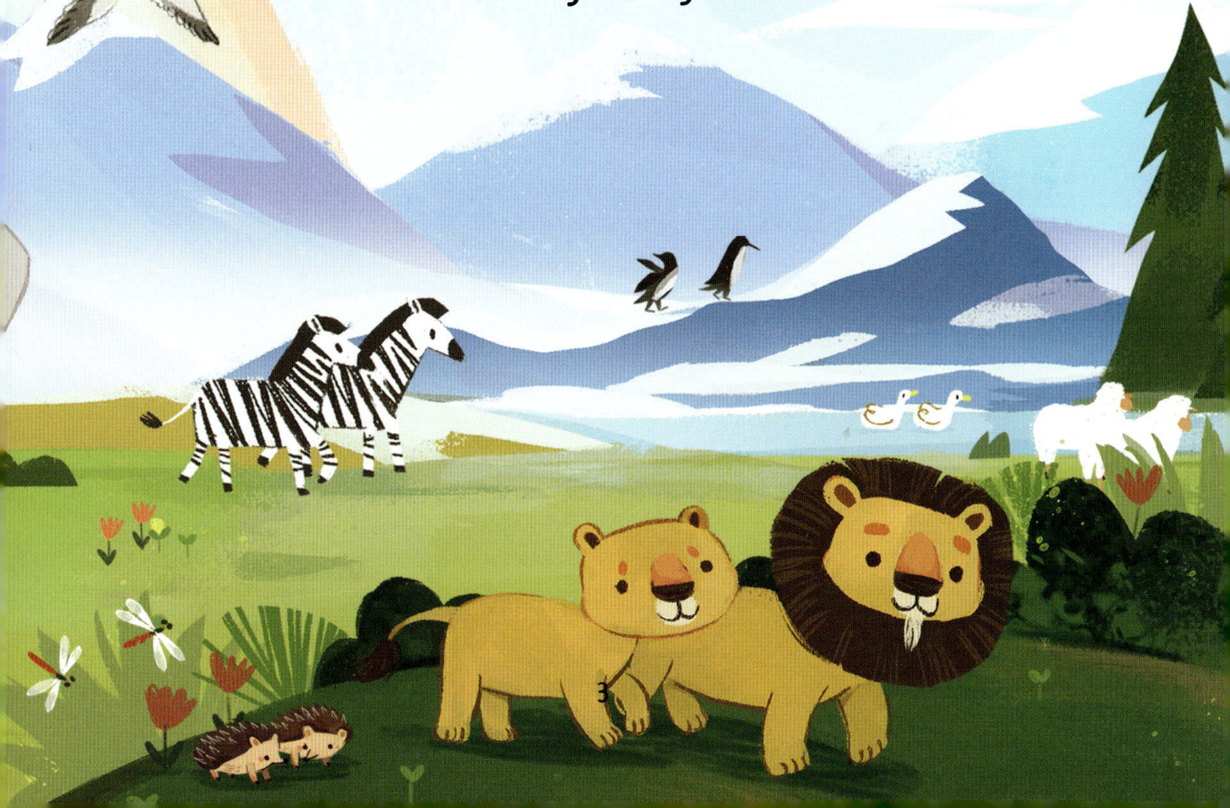

Contents

About the Bible — 6

Noah's Ark — 9
Illustrated by BlueBean

Joseph and his Wonderful Coat — 37
Illustrated by Héloïse Mab

The Baby in the Basket — 65
Illustrated by Katya Longhi

David and Goliath 85
Illustrated by Erin Brown

Jonah and the Great Big Fish 109
Illustrated by Corinne Caro

Daniel in the Lions' Den 135
Illustrated by Can Tuğrul

Map of Bible Lands 159

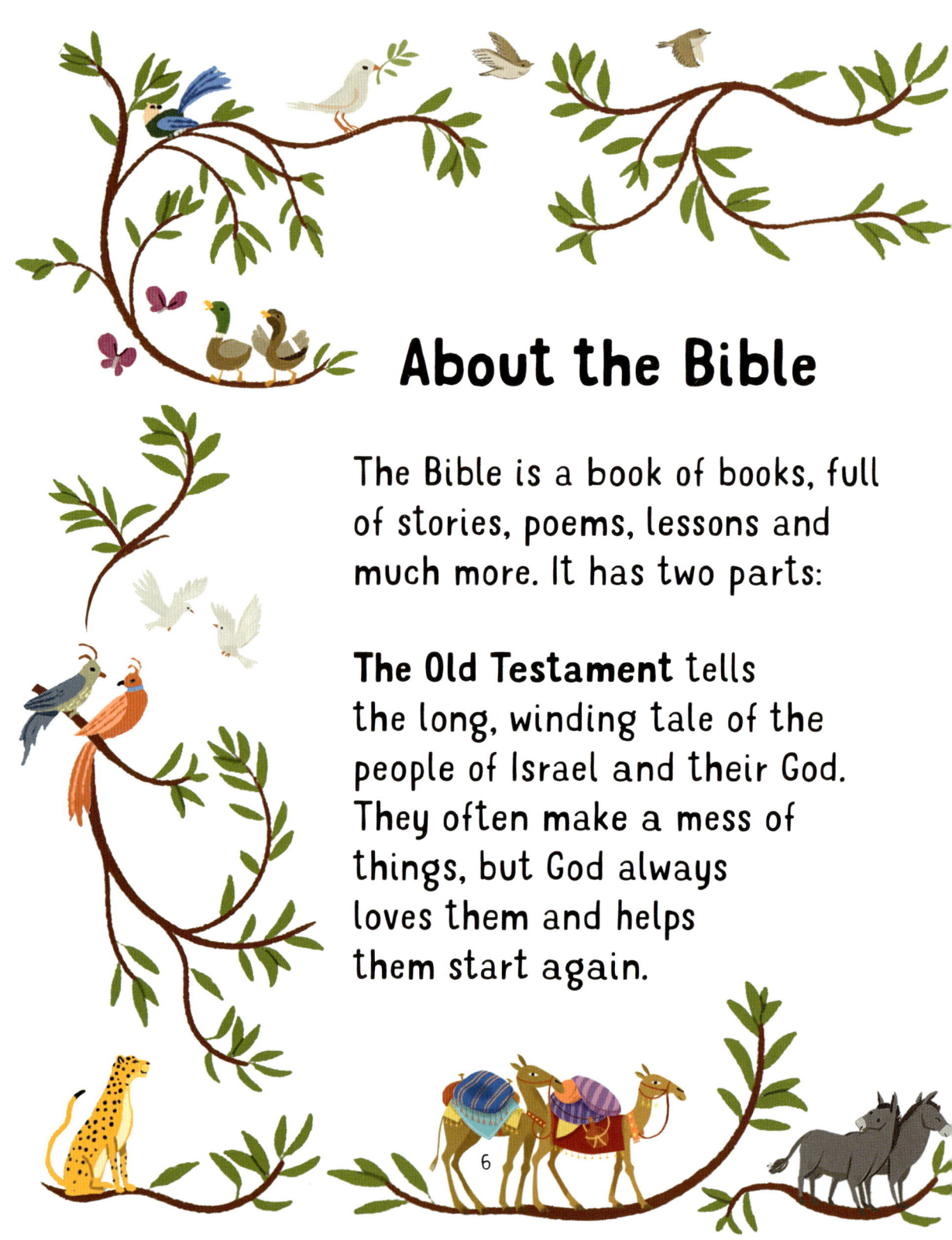

About the Bible

The Bible is a book of books, full of stories, poems, lessons and much more. It has two parts:

The Old Testament tells the long, winding tale of the people of Israel and their God. They often make a mess of things, but God always loves them and helps them start again.

The New Testament is the story of Jesus Christ, and of those who believed he was God's Son. He showed them in person what God is like.

The six stories in this book are from the Old Testament. You'll read about people with big problems, from jealous brothers to a terrifying giant. But they all discover that with God, nothing is impossible.

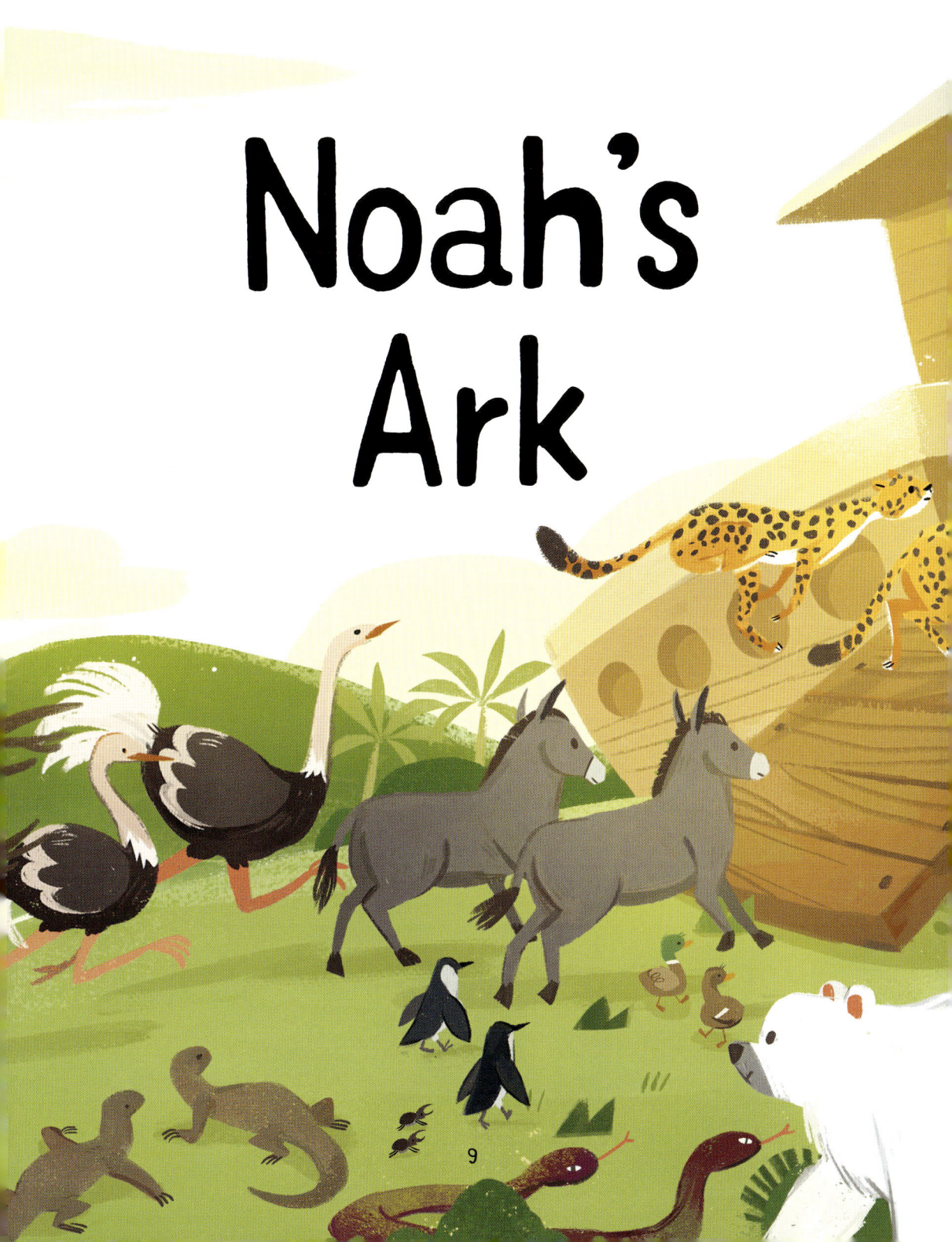

Once, a long, long time ago, God looked out upon the Earth. He had made a beautiful home for every living thing.

But something had gone wrong. Very, *very* wrong.

People had filled the Earth with hurt and hate.

And it broke God's heart.

No one listened to God
except a man named Noah.

Noah did what was right and good,
and he made God smile.

One day, God spoke to him.

"Noah, I am going to send a great flood to wash everyone away.

But you and all your family will be safe.

And Noah, I have a job for you…

…a very BIG job."

...room for two of each kind of animal under the sun.

Don't forget to pack plenty of food."

So Noah got to work.

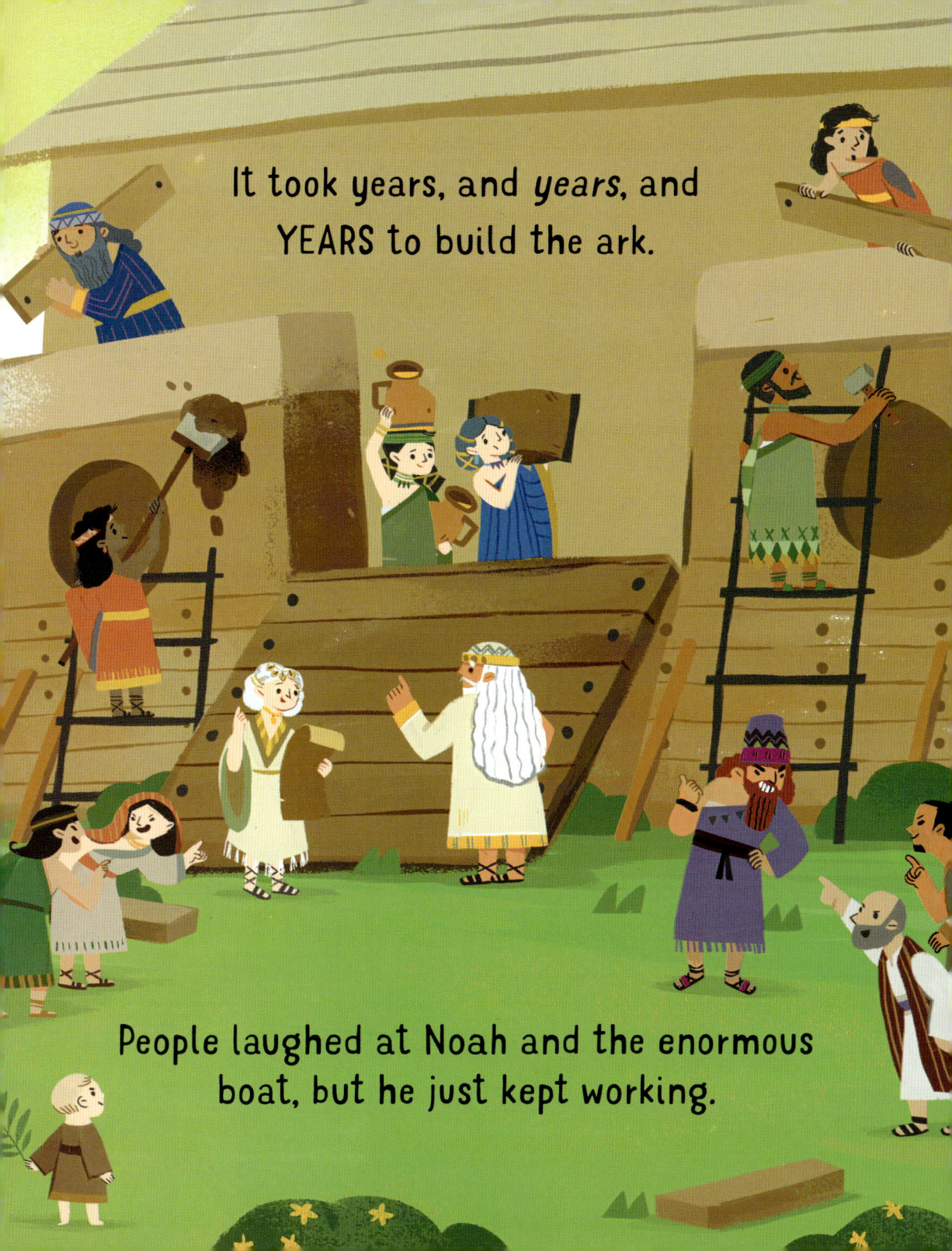

Finally, the ark was finished.

God spoke again.

"Noah, the time has come to go into the ark."

Animals! Animals of every kind, heading towards them, two by two...

Fluttering butterflies, birds on the wing and every sort of flying thing.

Loping and thundering, beasts of the land, with hooves and with horns, with claws and with fangs.

Skittering beetles and lizards that dart, all that wiggles or slithers, they entered the ark.

When the very last creatures were safely inside, God shut the door.

They waited...

...and they waited...

Everything was washed away as the ark rocked and swayed in the raging flood.

On the forty-first day, the rain stopped.

For five months, the world was lost underwater. Noah and his family took care of all the animals.

Then, with a bump and a scrape, the ark came to rest on a mountain.

So Noah let out a dove.

Finding nowhere to rest, it flew back to him.

Seven days later, he sent it out again.

That evening, the dove returned with a sprig of fresh olive leaves in its beak.

After another seven days,
Noah sent it out once more...

A week went by, and there was no sign of the dove. Now Noah knew it had found a home and the land was dry again.

Noah and his family celebrated. The animals roared and trumpeted, grunted and growled, warbled, squeaked, clucked and howled.

Joyfully, and two by two, they poured out into God's fresh, green, beautiful new world.

Then God blessed Noah, his family and all the animals, and declared...

"Never again will I end the world with a flood. Every rainbow you see will remind you of my promise, forever."

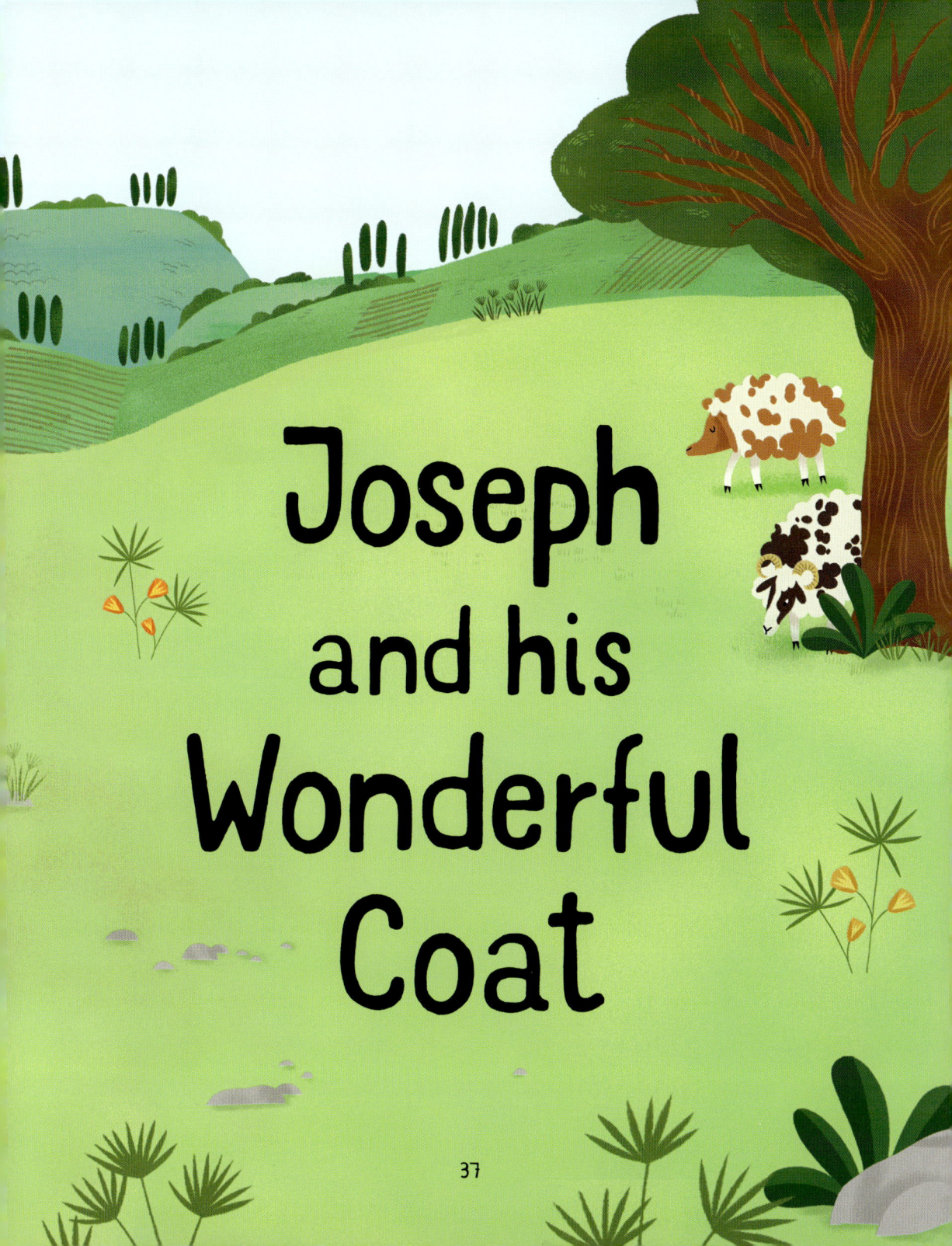

Joseph lived with his family
in the land of Canaan.

His father, Jacob, had many children
but he loved Joseph most of all.

One day, Jacob gave Joseph the most wonderful coat anyone had ever seen.

His jealous brothers started to hate him.

Joseph's dreams were amazing, too.

I dreamed that it was harvest time...

...and all your wheat sheaves bowed to mine!

"He thinks he's better than us!" grumbled his brothers.

His spiteful brothers tore off his coat and sold him to passing traders.

But I'm your brother!

They ripped and slashed his coat,
and showed it to Jacob.

*My poor son is dead!
Savaged by some wild beast!*

The old man was heartbroken.

Meanwhile, after ten days of tiring travel, the traders arrived in Egypt...

...and sold Joseph to a wealthy man named Potiphar.

But God was watching over him. Joseph impressed his master. Soon he was running the house.

For ten years, all went well.

Then Potiphar's wicked wife told her husband a terrible lie:

Furious, Potiphar threw Joseph in jail.

But God was still watching over him.
Joseph impressed the warden and
soon he was running the jail.

He was kind to everyone.
He even told prisoners the
meaning of their dreams.

This went on
for three long years...

One night, the Pharaoh himself, the King of Egypt, was disturbed by puzzling dreams...

He saw seven fat cows and seven thin cows climb out of the River Nile.

"The thin cows ate the fat ones, but stayed just as skinny," said the Pharaoh, with a frown.

What can this mean?

Even his wisest advisers were baffled.

"Your Majesty, why not ask Potiphar's slave, Joseph?" suggested a trusty servant. "People say he can read dreams."

"Bring me this Joseph!" roared the Pharaoh.

"AT ONCE!"

The guards whisked Joseph out of jail and marched him to the king.

"Great Pharaoh," Joseph began,
"these dreams are a message from God."

For seven years there will be plenty of food...
...but seven years of terrible harvests will follow.

"I suggest you find a wise man to store up
spare food for the hard times to come."

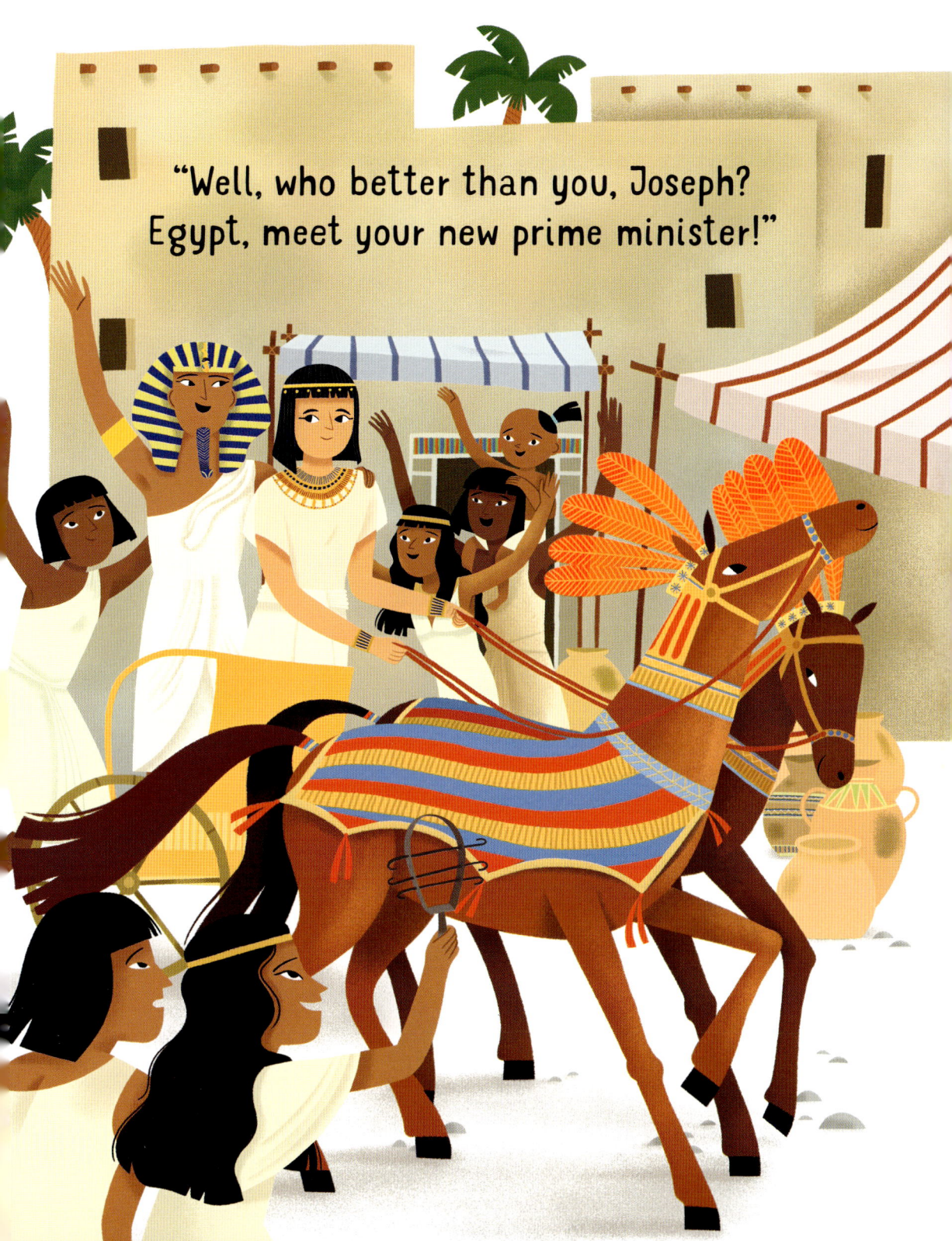

All that Joseph said came true.

For seven years, the harvests were HUGE. Joseph stored up all the extra grain.

When the harvests failed, Egypt had plenty of food to spare.

This barn has enough for three months.

Joseph decided to test his brothers.
He invited them all to a splendid feast.

Then he sent them home with sacks and bags bursting with wheat — and an extra surprise hidden inside.

As the brothers went on their way,
Joseph's servants ran after them.
"STOP!" roared one. "THIEVES!"

Search their bags!

The brothers trudged back to the palace, scared of what might happen.

"We were so mean to Joseph," sighed one. "I'm sure God is paying us back with this trouble."

Trembling like wheat in the wind, they stood before Joseph and bowed very low...

"You **STOLE** from me?" Joseph thundered at Benjamin, trying to sound as angry as he could.

When Joseph saw them protect
Benjamin, he burst into tears.
"I can't pretend any longer!" he said.

It's me, Joseph!

"Don't be afraid," he reassured
his shocked brothers. "I forgive you all."

Joseph moved his whole family to Egypt. When Jacob arrived, Joseph raced out to meet him, his arms open wide.

Jacob wiped away tears of joy. "I have my son back at last!"

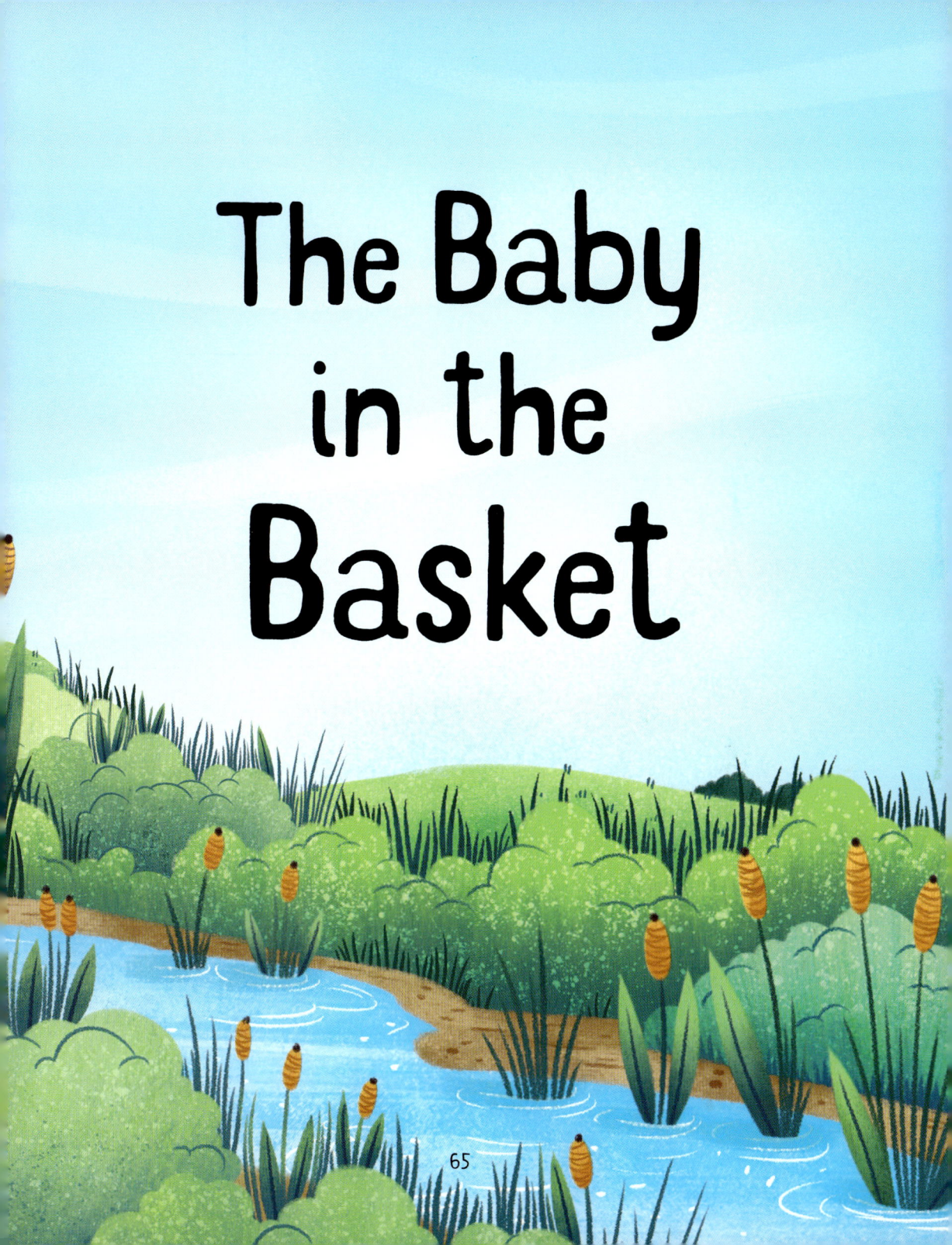

The Israelites had lived peacefully with the Egyptians for hundreds of years.

God blessed them and their families grew bigger and BIGGER.

One day, a new Pharaoh took the throne.
He was scared of the Israelites.

"There are too many of them!" he growled.
"What if they turn against us?"

I'll put them in their place!

So the Pharaoh forced the Israelites to work as slaves.

But the harder he worked them, the more God blessed them. Soon they had more babies than the Egyptians.

Miriam was an Israelite girl who lived in Egypt with...

...her mother and father...

...her younger brother, Aaron...

...and their brand new baby brother.

When they heard about the new law, they were HORRIFIED. They all tried to keep the baby hidden...

So, early one morning, Miriam and her mother snuggled the baby in a basket and carried him to the River Nile.

Don't worry, little one!

The basket was light, but their hearts were heavy.

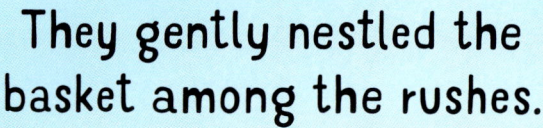

They gently nestled the basket among the rushes.

Please, God, may this little boat keep our baby safe.

Slowly and sadly, Miriam's mother walked back to the house.

Miriam kept watch nearby.

Then she heard voices. *Who could it be?*

Miriam gasped. It was the Pharaoh's daughter and her maids.

The princess spied the basket and sent a maid to fetch it.

Burning with curiosity, she peeked inside.

"It's one of those poor Israelite boys. Whatever can I do for him?"

Miriam saw her chance. With a deep breath, she approached the princess.

"P-pardon me, Your Highness," she said, "Shall I find an Israelite woman to care for him?"

I know someone who could help.

The princess smiled. "What a good idea!"

At last, the princess called Miriam's mother and brother to the palace.

"I will care for him now," she declared. "And I shall name him Moses."

The princess adopted Moses
and he grew up as a prince of Egypt...

...but he never forgot he was an Israelite too.

David and Goliath

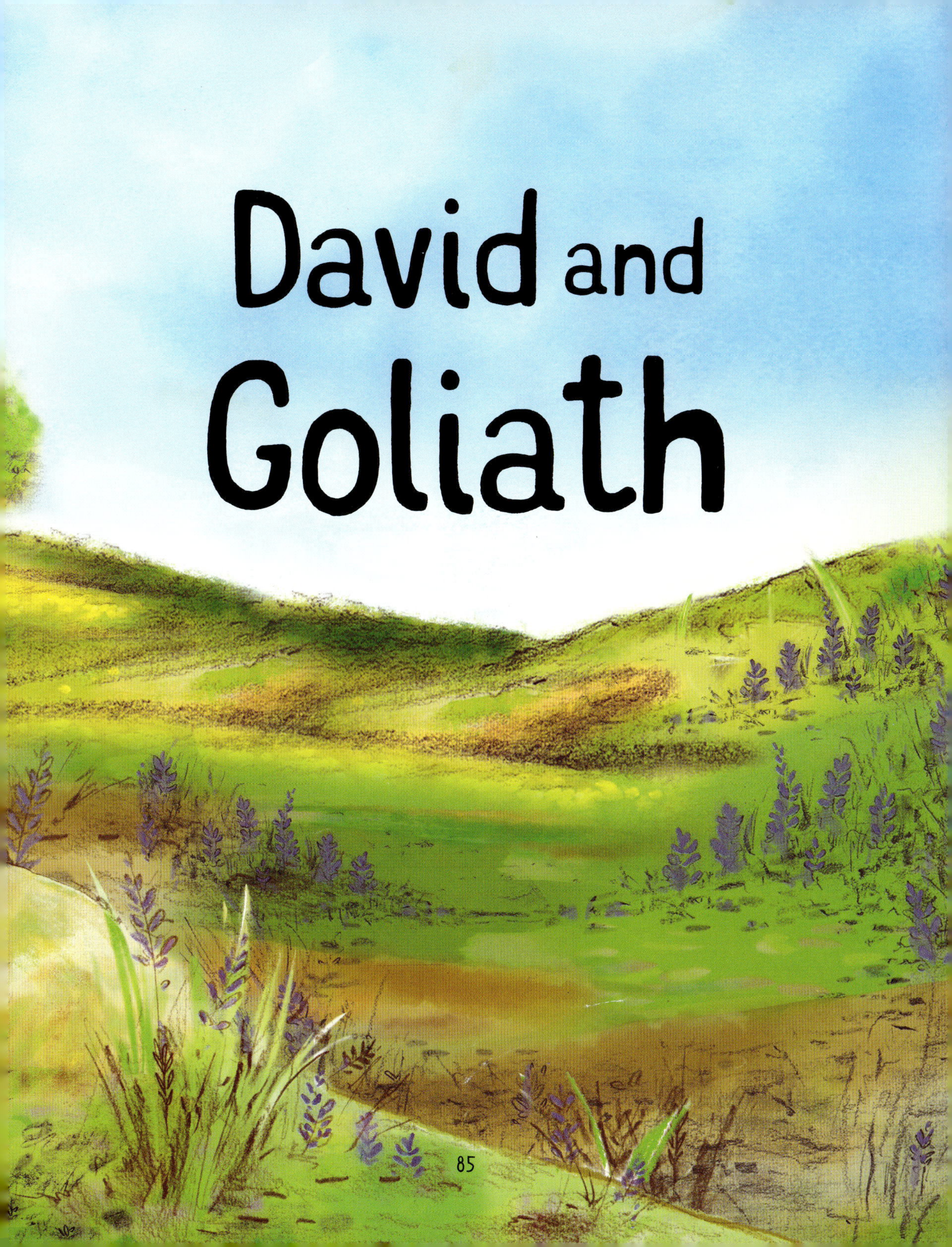

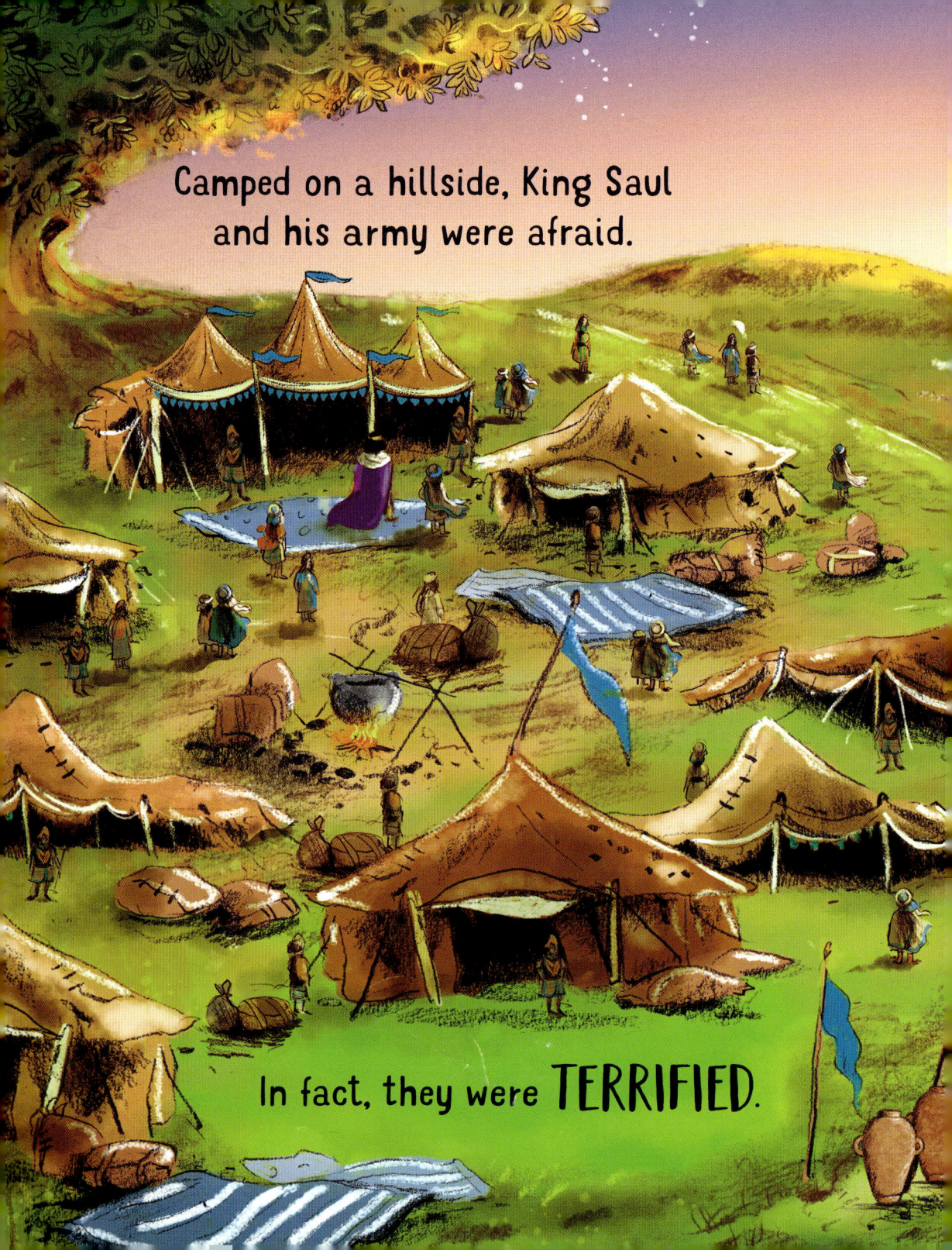

His name was Goliath, and he was

ENORMOUS!

He wore a helmet of gleaming bronze.

His tunic was as heavy as a man,
its scales glinting and rattling
like a deadly desert snake.

Day after day, Goliath strode out to the battlefield.

"Is there a man among you brave enough to face ME?" he roared.

If he can beat me, we will become your slaves.

But if I win, we will make slaves out of YOU!

No one would face the giant.
King Saul and his army were frozen in fear.

Each day he led the sheep to food and water.

And each night he kept them safe from wild beasts.

One day, David took lunch
to his three eldest brothers,
who served in Saul's army.

The trembling soldiers
were lining up for battle.

"You're a joke!" mocked Goliath. "If you won't fight me, why line up at all?"

The soldiers shrank back, but David was furious.

But King Saul heard about the boast and summoned David to his tent.

Don't worry, Sire. I will fight Goliath!

You're just a boy, David.

Instead, David went to the river
and chose five smooth pebbles.

Clutching his stick and catapult,
he headed back to the battlefield.

But David wasn't afraid.

God will help me!

Goliath toppled like a tree and **Crashed** to the ground.

When the Philistines saw their champion fall, they panicked.

With whoops of victory, King Saul's army chased them away.

David was a hero!

Hurray for David!

You know, one day that boy could be a king...

Jonah and the Great Big Fish

One day, God gave him a new message.

"Go to the city of Nineveh. Tell its wicked people I will punish them. They must change their ways."

But the people of Nineveh were enemies of the Israelites. Jonah didn't want to go...

...so he decided to sail far away.

The captain rushed down to Jonah, who was snoring... **loudly.**

ZZZZZz...

Wake up! Wake up! Can **your** god help us?

Now the sailors were terrified.

"This is my fault!" yelled Jonah. "I tried to run away from God. Throw me overboard and the storm will stop."

"We can't do that!" cried the sailors.

But the storm raged stronger than ever, and they knew they had no choice.

As soon as Jonah hit the waves,
the clouds parted and the sea grew still.

Down went Jonah beneath the waves... deeper and deeper until the darkness swallowed him.

To Jonah's surprise, he wasn't dead...

...but inside a great **big fish!**

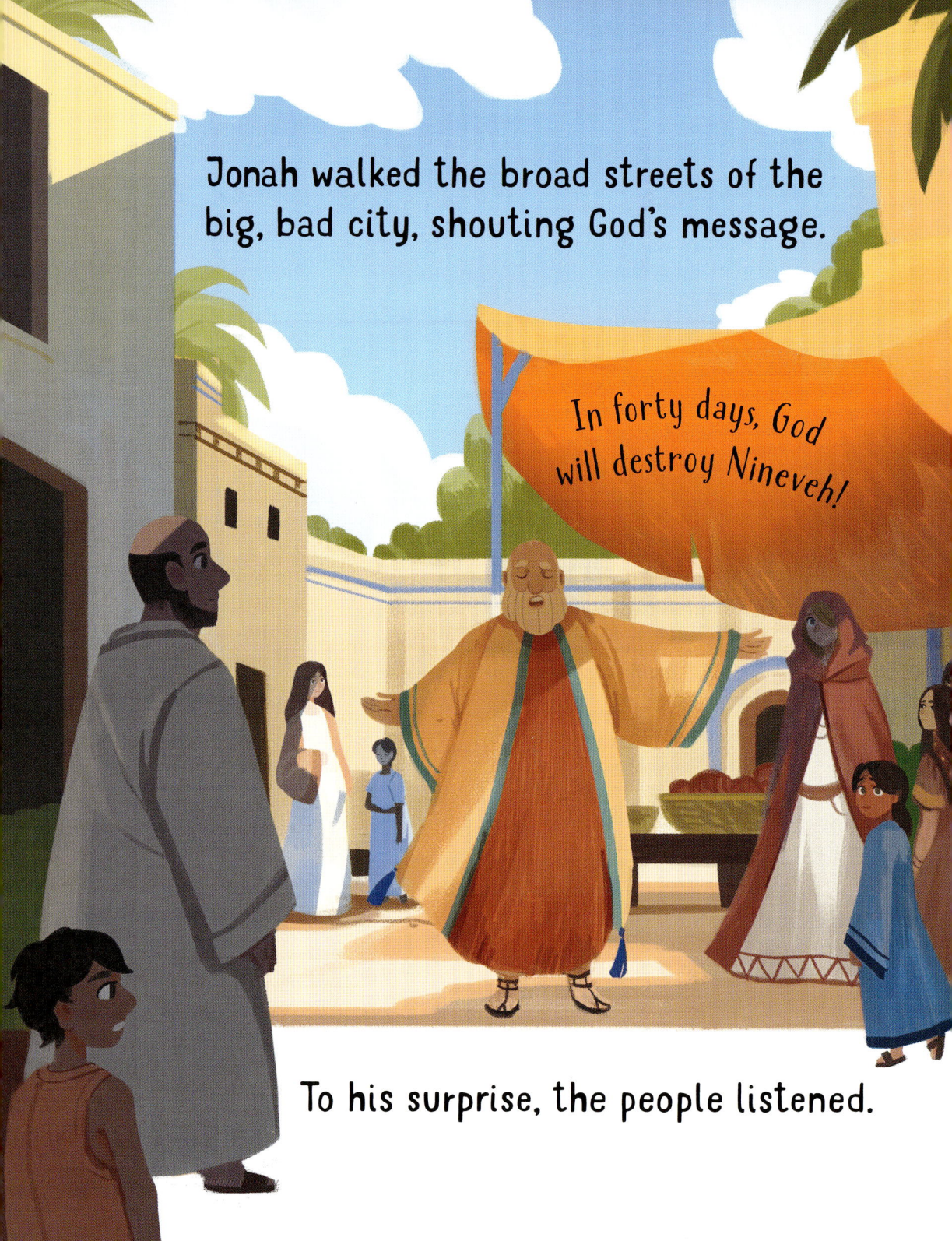

The King of Nineveh was so sorry for his wickedness that he stopped eating.

He gave up sitting on his grand throne and started wearing old sacks.

Then he ordered everyone to do the same — even the animals! They all prayed to God.

When God saw that they had changed their ways, he forgave them.

Jonah was **FURIOUS!**

"How can you forgive them?" he bellowed.
"These people are my **ENEMY!**"

God spoke gently.

"I am good and fair, Jonah.

I love all that I have made — including the people of Nineveh and their animals too. And I forgive anyone who is truly sorry."

Daniel in the Lions' Den

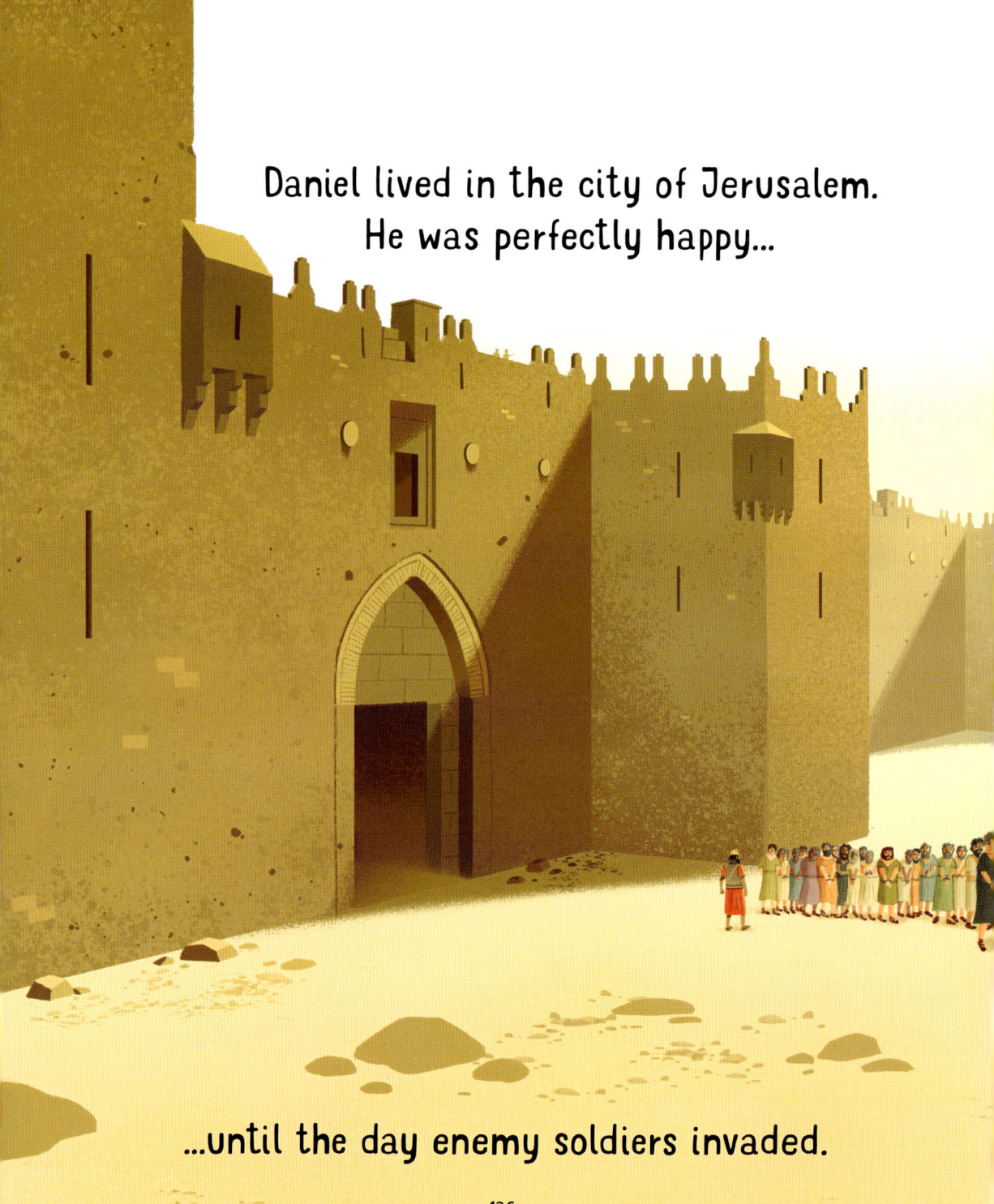

Daniel lived in the city of Jerusalem. He was perfectly happy...

...until the day enemy soldiers invaded.

They captured Daniel and his friends and marched them far, far away...

Daniel went to school every day...

...and prayed to God every morning, noon and night.

Daniel grew into a wise man.
Even the king asked his advice.

I had the strangest dream about a tree!
What can it mean?

So did the kings who ruled after him.

One day, King Darius came to power.
He put three men in charge of his
kingdom — and Daniel was one.

Daniel did a **much** better job than the other two —
even when he was collecting money.

So Darius put Daniel in charge of everyone.

The other chiefs grew crazed with jealousy, and started to plot against Daniel.

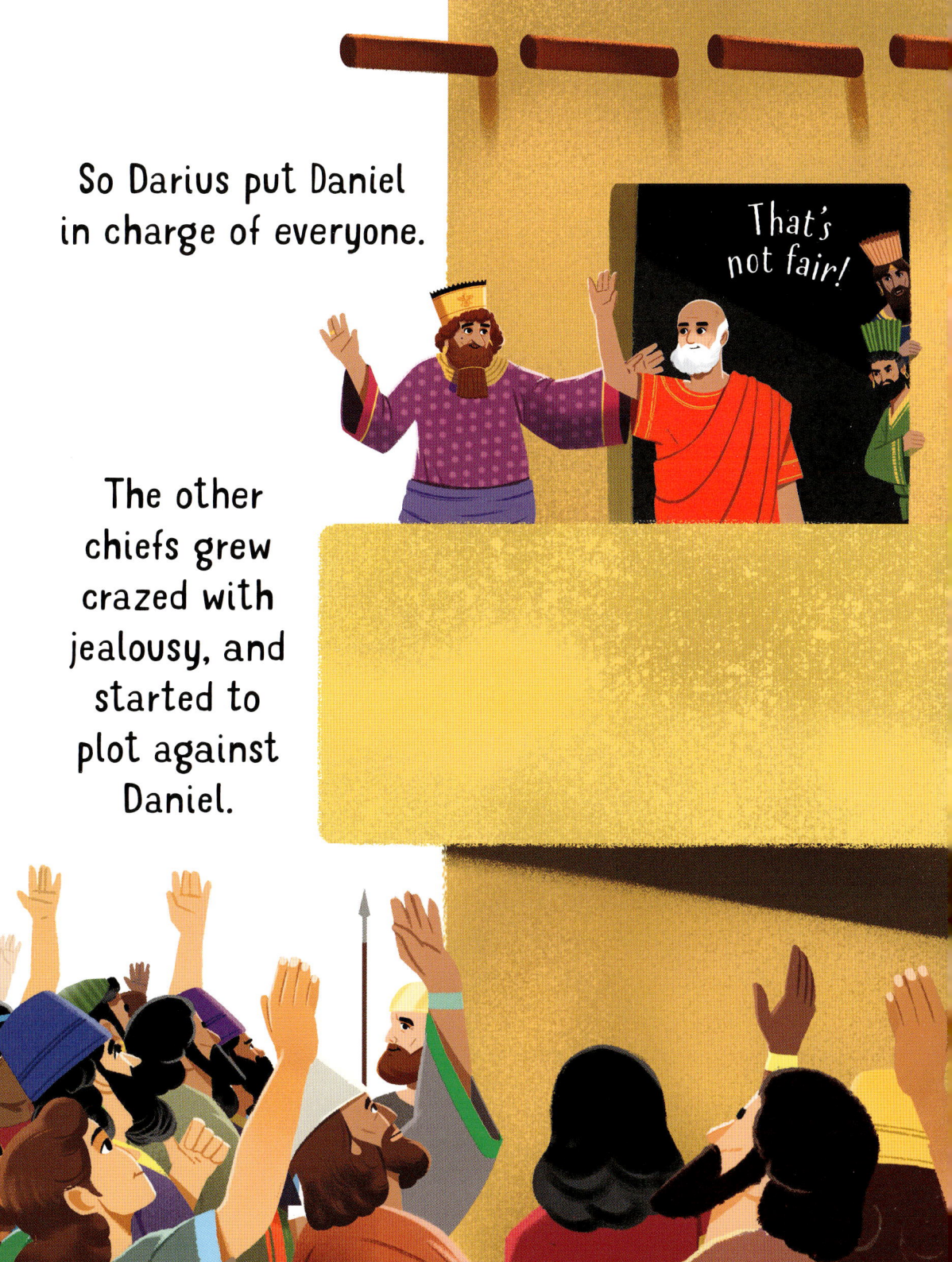

The chiefs hurried to the king
and bowed low before him.

"O mighty Darius, may you live forever!
We've had a wonderful idea," they said.

"Why not make a new law?
Everyone must pray to **YOU**
and only you for thirty days —
or be thrown into the lions' den."

Puffing out his chest with pride,
the king agreed.

When Daniel heard about the law, he knew at once the chiefs were behind it.

But he trusted in God, and kept on praying three times a day.

That evening, Daniel's enemies crept to his house. There he stood, saying his prayers for all to see.

Aha! Now he'll be sorry!

The chiefs ran straight to the king with their news. Darius was upset and angry. "I forgot Daniel prayed to his god..."

They tricked me with their new law!

He spent all day looking for a way to save Daniel, but there was nothing he could do.

"A law is a law," sighed Darius and gave the order.

Take Daniel to the lions.

Darius walked beside Daniel, trying to give him hope.

But he didn't really believe Daniel would survive.

Hair-raising growls filled the air, as stern-faced guards slowly lowered Daniel into the lions' den. Then they rolled a heavy stone across the hole.

Silently, Darius walked away.

Darius felt dreadful.
He was too worried to eat.
Nothing could cheer him up.

That night, he did not sleep a wink.

As soon as the sun came up,
Darius rushed to the lion pit.
"Roll back the stone!" he cried.

"Daniel!" he shouted.
"Did your god rescue you?"

The king was overjoyed. He shouted, "Bring Daniel out at once!"

That very day, the king sent out this message to his people:

May you all be filled with peace, health and happiness!

Everyone must pray to the god of Daniel, who saved him from the lions' jaws!

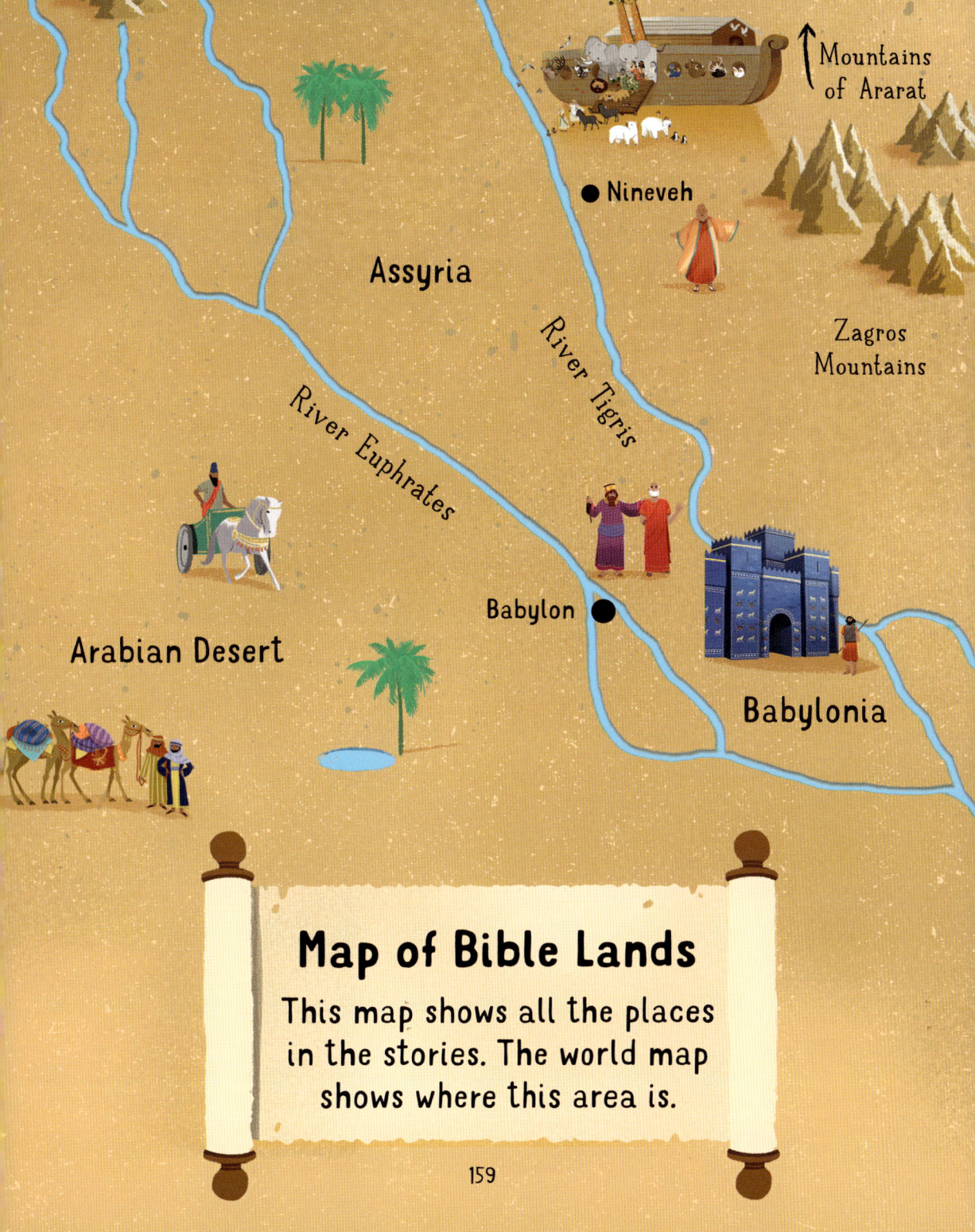

Digital imaging: Nick Wakeford
and Hope Reynolds
Series designer: Russell Punter
Series editor: Lesley Sims

First published in 2023 by Usborne Publishing Limited, 83-85 Saffron Hill, London EC1N 8RT, United Kingdom. usborne.com Copyright © 2023 Usborne Publishing Limited. The name Usborne and the Balloon logo are registered trade marks of Usborne Publishing Limited. All rights reserved. No part of this publication may be reproduced, stored in a retrieval system, or transmitted in any form or by any means, without prior permission of the publisher. UE. First published in America 2023.